Also By Frank McClain

YOU'RE HIRED!

Winner of the **Independent Book Publishers Association 2017 *Benjamin Franklin Digital Award***. Success secrets to phone and in-person job interviews for job seekers and career changers.

IT Questions & Answers For IT Job Interviews, Volume 1

General IT Knowledge, Transmission Lines and Cabling,
Voice over IP (VoIP), Video and Telepresence over IP, Wireless (WiFi)

IT Questions & Answers For IT Job Interviews, Volume 2

IPv4 and IPv6 Addressing, NAT, Layer 2 Switching Concepts,
Layer 3 Routing Concepts

IT Questions & Answers For IT Job Interviews, Volume 3

BGP Routing, EIGRP Routing, OSPF Routing

IT Questions & Answers For IT Job Interviews, Volume 4

Data Center and Virtualization, F5 Networks Load Balancer,
Riverbed WAN Optimization

IT Questions & Answers For IT Job Interviews, Volume 5

Access Lists and Prefix Lists, Tunnels and VPNs, Cisco ASA Firewall

IT Questions & Answers For IT Job Interviews, Volume 6

Service Provider Networks, Quality of Service (QoS),
Troubleshooting Router and Switch Interfaces

Awards for Job Hunting Ninja Master

Job Hunting Ninja Master 2017 won the **Foreword Reviews'** prestigious **2016 Foreword INDIES Book of the Year Award**. In a competition with over 1500 other entrants whose books were judged by a panel of over 150 judges made up of librarians and booksellers reading every page, the judges chose *Job Hunting Ninja Master 2017* as a winner of the **Book of the Year** for job hunters.

"Being an INDIES winner is no small feat—particularly this year when there was a record number of entries." – **INDIES Awards Director**

****

The multi-award-winning *Job Hunting Ninja Master 2017* is rated "Best in Class" by winning the **Independent Book Publishers Association 2017 *Benjamin Franklin Digital Award***.

"Well written . . . exceeds user expectations very well . . . the book is well organized and develops the subject matter in great detail . . . the use of links to additional material was very useful and well done . . . follows generally accepted principles of good writing for the genre very well . . . grammar, spelling, punctuation, etc. is very well" – **IBPA Benjamin Franklin Digital Award Judge**

Praise for Job Hunting Ninja Master

"Your book exceeded my expectations! . . . I was impressed by the amount of specific details in this book. I thought I had a fair amount of experience in the job seeking process, but I learned a lot of useful things in this book. I wish I had this information earlier." - **Ali Julia, Top 10 Amazon Reviewer**

Job Hunting Ninja Master 2017

The art of job searching, resumes, interviews and negotiating salary for US government and corporate jobs

Frank McClain

Copyright © 2016 by Frank McClain

All Rights Reserved. No part of this publication may be reproduced, stored in a retrieval system, or transmitted, in any form or by any means—electronic, mechanical, photocopying, recording, or otherwise—without prior written permission except in the case of brief quotations embodied in critical articles and reviews.

Publisher's Note. This publication is designed to provide accurate and authoritative information in regard to the subject matter. It is sold with the understanding that the publisher is not engaged in rendering professional career, legal, financial, psychological or health services. If expert assistance is required, the service of the appropriate professional should be sought.

Edited by Clarence Z. Seacrest

Cover design by www.the.designfairies.com

ISBN 978-0-9982384-0-1 (paperback)
ISBN 978-0-9982384-1-8 (hardcover)
ISBN 978-0-9982384-2-5 (ebook)

Dedication

To my Lord and Savior Jesus Christ. Surely Your goodness, mercy and unfailing love have followed me all the days of my life. ~ Psalm 23

To my step-father, Balbino Rodriguez, a true American patriot who served our country in the US Navy for 27 years; served during World War II; and survived the bombing attack on Pearl Harbor. He was a Navy chef for President Franklin D. Roosevelt on the presidential yacht, the USS Potomac, while our country's 32nd president led our nation through World War II and out of the Great Depression. He was also a Navy chef for President Harry S. Truman on the presidential yacht, the USS Williamsburg, while the White House was undergoing extensive restoration; and while President Truman brought our nation out of World War II with a decisive victory, and through our nation's turbulent times of the Cold War and the Korean War. My step-dad remained a faithful and loving husband to my mother, Dolores, for 37 years until his death at 106 years of age. But above all of this, he was the best father a son could ever dream of having.

To the U.S. Air Force where I served 20 years in the greatest air force in the world. The Air Force taught me the value of sacrifice, hard work, commitment and service before self to our great country. It has been my highest honor to be a part of the greatest military in the world while serving our great country in the U.S. Air Force. *Aim High*!

Table of Contents

DEDICATION vi

TABLE OF CONTENTS vii

INTRODUCTION xix

CHAPTER ONE: SOMETHING FOR EVERY JOB SEEKER 1
- Life is a Competition 3
- The Warm-Up before the Competition 4
- **Employees and Contractors** 5
  - Independent Contractors versus Dependent Contractors 7
- **Direct Hire, Contract-to-Hire or Contract** 9
  - Direct Hire Worker 9
  - Contract-to-Hire Worker 12
  - Contract Worker 19
- **W-2, W-4, W-9, 1099 and Corp-to-Corp Tax Forms** 19
  - Working under a W-2 19
  - Working under a W-4 20
  - Working under a 1099 or Corp-to-Corp (C2C) 20
  - Working under a 1099 21
  - Working under a Corp-to-Corp (C2C) 23
  - Using Tax Status as Leverage to Negotiate Your Salary with Staffing Agencies and Company Clients 23
- **Working Hours** 25
  - Out of the Mouths of Babes 25
  - Fair Labor Standards Act (FLSA) and the 40-Hour Workweek 26
  - Full-Time and Part-Time Hours 27
  - Wages for Alternative Working Hours 28
  - Using Odd Working Hours as Leverage to Increase Your Salary 29
- **Seasonal or Holiday Jobs** 30
  - Ride the Wave of Seasonal Hiring 30

Catch the Holiday Wave of Hiring	32
Where to Look For Holiday Jobs	34
Dress for Success When Applying for Seasonal Jobs	36
Exempt versus Non-Exempt Employees	**36**
Using Overtime as Leverage to Increase your Salary	39
Stupid is What Stupid Does	40
Salary Workers versus Hourly Workers	**44**
Salary Workers	44
Hourly Workers	45
Salary and Hourly Positions Offered by Recruiters	45
Company Benefits	**46**
Using Company Benefits as Leverage to Increase Your Salary	47
Business Travel	**49**
Pros to Business Travel	50
Cons to Business Travel	50
Living and Working Overseas	**51**
Take a Selfie in Europe	51
Expatriates	53
Foreign Earned Income Exclusion for Expatriates	55
Paying Income Tax to a Foreign Country	57
Pros to Living and Working Overseas	59
Cons to Living and Working Overseas	61
Resources for Finding Overseas Jobs and Living Overseas	63
Contractor Jobs in Austere, Danger/Hazard Overseas Areas	**67**
Not a Griswold's European Vacation	67
Defense Contractor Jobs in Austere, Danger/Hazard Areas	68
Salaries and Benefits of Defense Contractors Working in Austere, Danger/Hazard Locations	69
Hardship Pay for Working in Auster, Danger/Hazard Locations	73
Completion Bonus for Working in Auster, Danger/Hazard Locations	73
Using Leverage to Increase your Salary or Benefits for Austere, Danger/Hazard Overseas Locations	74
Living Quarters, Food and Services for Defense Contractors Working in Austere, Danger/Hazard Overseas Locations	75
Living Outside the Military Installation in Auster, Danger/Hazard Locations	76

Living Inside the Military Installation in Auster, Danger/Hazard Locations	77
Dining Facility and Other Services on the Military Installation	79
Staying Connected to Family and Friends While Deployed in Austere, Danger/Hazard Overseas Locations	80
Medical, Training, Equipment and Other Requirements for Contractors Headed to Austere, Danger/Hazard Locations	82
CONUS Replacement Center (CRC)	83
Lodging and Transportation at Fort Bliss, Texas	84
Meals at Fort Bliss, Texas	85
Medical, Dental and Physical Examination Requirements for CRC Processing	85
CRC Training Requirements	92
"No Go" Rosters and Employer Communications at the CRC	95
Common Access Card (CAC)—Your Total Access Card	96
Equipment Issued to You at the CRC	98
Flights to Your Overseas Locations	100
Baggage Allowed for Your Flight to Your Overseas Location	100
Thank You Sir, May I Have Another?	101
US Training Center in Moyock, North Carolina	102
Lodging at the US Training Center	103
Meals at the US Training Center	103
Common Access Card (CAC)—Your Total Access Card	106
Baggage Allowed and Flights for Your Trip to Your Overseas Location	106
Cleanup and Recovery after Hurricane Matthew	107
Employer-Hosted Training or Processing for Overseas Locations	108
Taking Care of Things Before You Leave for Your Training Center	109
Resources for Finding Defense Contractor Jobs in Austere, Danger/Hazard Locations	111
CHAPTER TWO: US GOVERNMENT EMPLOYEE AND CONTRACTOR WORKFORCE	113
US Government Employees—Who We Are	113
Military Veterans and Their Family Members as US Government Employees and Contractors	114
The Department of Defense (DoD)	116

Life and the Working Environment within US Government Organizations 116
Restrictions on What You Can Bring Into a US Government Agency 118
Consequences of Violating US Government Agency Policies 118
Military Exercises at US Military Installations 119
The Office of Personnel Management (OPM) 120

Salaries of US Government Employees 121

The General Schedule (GS) Pay System 122
Base Pay and Locality Pay in the GS Pay System 122
Cost of Living Allowance (COLA) in the GS Pay System 123
Special Pay Rates for US Government Jobs 124
Military Veterans Working Overseas as US Government Employees 127
Grade Level and Step Level in the GS Pay System 127
The Grade Level 128
The Step Level 129
The Grade-Step Level Matrix in the GS Pay System 130
Negotiating Your Salary in the GS Pay System 131
Conversion of the GS Pay System to the National Security Personnel System (NSPS) and the Acquisition Demonstration Project (AcqDemo) Pay Systems 132
National Security Personnel System (NSPS) 132
Acquisition Workforce Personnel Demonstration Project (AcqDemo) 134

Company Benefits for US Government Employees 137

The Civil Service Retirement System (CSRS) 137
The Federal Employees Retirement System (FERS) 138
The Thrift Savings Plan 139

The Application Process for US Government Employee Jobs 140

Welcome to Jurassic Park 140
What Doesn't Kill You Makes You Stronger 140
The USAJOBS and Other Websites for US Government Jobs 141
Knowledge, Skills and Abilities (KSA) Questionnaire 145
Resumes for US Government Employee Jobs 146
The Validity Coefficient—the Threshold for Your Selection 147
The US Government's Assessment Decision Tool (ADT) 148
The Waiting Period and Status after Submitting Your Application for US Government Employee Jobs 148

US Government Contractors—Who We Are 149

Salaries of US Government Contractors	150
The Application Process for US Government Contractor Jobs	153
Welcome to Disneyland Park	153
To Be or Not to Be a US Government Employee or Contractor	154
US Government Contracts with Private Companies	155
When Another Company Wins the US Government Contract	156
Job Opportunities for Contractors during the Government Agency Bidding Process	159
The Choice is Yours	160
CHAPTER THREE: SECURITY CLEARANCES AND TRAINING	163
What Are US Government Security Clearances	163
Sensitive Compartmented Information (SCI)	164
Single Scope Background Investigation (SSBI)	165
When Are Security Clearances Needed	165
How Long Are Security Clearances Valid	166
Obtaining a US Government Security Clearance	167
Joint Personnel Adjudication System (JPAS)	168
Applying for a Security Clearance	168
Interim Security Clearance—Your Foot in the Door	171
Security Clearance Adjudication—the Final Decision	172
Getting Employers to Submit You for a Security Clearance	172
Job-Hunting Advantages of Having a Security Clearance	174
Military Veterans and Security Clearances	175
Using Your Security Clearance	175
Security Training, Testing and Certification Requirements	176
Security Training and Testing	179
Security Certification Through Computing Technology Industry Association (CompTIA) Security+	181
CompTIA Continuing Education (CE) Program	181
Company Reimbursement for CompTIA CE Fees	183
Advantages of Security Certification for Job-Hunters	183

CHAPTER FOUR: CORPORATE EMPLOYEE AND CONTRACTOR WORKFORCE — 185

Who We Are — 185
Corporate Employee—Who We Are — 186
Corporate Contractor—Who We Are — 186
- Independent Contractors — 186
- Dependent Contractors — 187
- Job-Hoppers and Jumpers — 187
- Contractors are Free Agents — 188
- Contractors in the Corporate World — 190

Private Companies, Businesses and Organizations — 191
- Time To Choose — 193

CHAPTER FIVE: THE PERFECT RESUME — 195

Resume + Recruiter = Job Interview — 195
- The Curriculum Vitae (CV) and Resume — 195

How Recruiters Review Your Resume — 196
- Make Recruiters Search for You Instead of You Searching for the Job — 197
- The Ladders Study on How Recruiters Review Your Resume — 198
- How Recruiters Use the Applicant Tracking System (ATS) to Find You — 201
- The Key to Getting a "Yes" from a Recruiter for Your Resume — 202
- The ATS System Looks for Keywords and Phrases in Resumes — 204
- What the ATS System Doesn't Like in Resumes — 206

Making Your Resume Stand Out to Recruiters and Hiring Managers — 207
- Using Positive Impact to Make Your Resume Stand Out — 207
- Action Verbs to Make Your Resume Stand Out — 211
- Attributes that Make You Stand Out to Hiring Managers — 212
- Have a Professional Write Your Resume — 213

Internet Job Search Websites — 214
- Update Your Resume Online To Attract Recruiters — 216

How Social Media Affects Your Job Opportunities — 218
Resume Reality Check — 221

CHAPTER SIX: DEALING WITH RECRUITERS — 225

Staffing Agencies — 225
The Recruiters — 226
- Retained and Contingency Recruiters — 226
- Retained Recruiters — 227
- Contingency Recruiters — 228
- Recruiter Alliances — 229
- The Recruiter's Commission — 229
- The Recruiter's Knowledge and Experience in Your Career Field — 230
- Be Wary of a Recruiter's Request for Your Resume — 231

The Good, the Bad and the Ugly Recruiter — 233
- Big Brother and Big Sister Recruiters (The Good) — 234
- Headhunter Recruiters (The Bad) — 236
- Dr. Jekyll and Mr. Hyde Recruiters (The Ugly) — 238
- Requests from Recruiters for Your Exclusive Rights Agreement — 241
- Submitting Multiple Resumes for the Same Job Opening — 251
- Don't Show All Your Cards to Recruiters — 252
- Requests from Recruiters to Visit Their Office — 253
- Requests from Recruiters for Your Personal Information — 255
- Requests from Recruiters for Your Job References — 258
- How to Manage Your Job References — 263

CHAPTER SEVEN: NEGOTIATING YOUR SALARY — 269

- If it's Not in Writing, it Never Happened — 270
- The Best Time to Increase Your Salary is When You're Job Hunting — 270
- You Decide What Your Salary Is — 271

Salary Negotiations Initiated by Recruiters — 273
- When the Recruiter Asks You What is Your Salary Expectation — 273
- A Specific Compensation is better than a Salary Range — 275
- When the Recruiter Tells You What the Salary Is — 277

Salary Negotiations Initiated by Job Candidates — 278
- Telling the Recruiter What Salary You Want — 280
- Asking the Recruiter What Salary the Employer is Willing to Pay — 281
- Ask For More Money — 282

Asking For More with Multiple Recruiters	287
Salary Negotiations Based on Other Factors	**289**
College Degrees versus Experience and Certifications	289
The Salary "Depends on Experience" Statement	291
HR, Hiring Managers and Staffing Agencies that Ask for Your Salary History	294
Why HR Departments and Hiring Managers Ask for Your Salary History	294
Why Staffing Agencies Ask for Your Salary History	296
Converting Between Annual Salary and Hourly Rate	**299**
Converting Annual Salary to Hourly Rate	299
Converting Hourly Rate to Annual Salary	300
It's All Fun and Games until Someone Gets Hurt	**301**
Negotiating Relocation Benefits	**302**
What are Relocation Benefits	302
Income Tax Exemptions for Job Relocations	303
CHAPTER EIGHT: JOB INTERVIEW PREPARATION AND TIPS	**309**
Start With a Thank You	310
First Impressions Are Lasting Impressions	310
Give Yourself Time to Prepare for the Job Interview	311
Appearance and Attire for Job Interviews	**314**
How Your Appearance and Attire Makes an Impression	314
How to Dress for Visits to Recruiter Offices	315
Prepare Your Attire Ahead of Time for the Job Interview	316
Research the Company Client	**322**
Research the Job Description	**328**
Employers Don't Expect You to Know Everything in the Job Description	328
The Job Description Reveals What Subjects the Interviewers Will Ask Questions About	329
Your Resume for the Job Interview	**330**
Your Resume Review Ensures Your Interviewers Have the Latest Version of Your Resume	330
Your Resume Review Ensures You Are Prepared to Talk About Your Resume	330
Certification's and Experience's Place in Job Interviews	**331**

Education's Place among Successful People	337
Success is Not Defined by Education	337
Successful People without a College Degree	338
Arrival at Your Job Interview	347
Introductions in Your Job Interview	348
How to Prepare Your Introduction for Your Job Interview	349
Technical Fitness and Cultural Fitness in Your Introduction	349
How to Include Your Technical Fitness in Your Introduction	351
How to Include Your Cultural Fitness in Your Introduction	352
Job Interview Questions and Answers	353
Job Interview Questions about Your Technical Fitness	354
Job Interview Questions about Your Cultural Fitness	355
How You Should Respond to the Weakness Question	356
Cultural Fitness Questions and Answers	359
Questions to Ask the Interviewers and Closure	370
Closing Statements at the End of Your Job Interview	375
Role-Playing Job Interviews	377
Practice Role-Playing with People You Know	377
Even the US Military Performs Job Interview Role-Playing for Their Departing Military Members	380
CHAPTER NINE: IT'S GAME DAY—THE JOB INTERVIEW	383
During the Job Interview	383
Everyone Gets a Little Nervous Before Game Day	383
The Job Interview Process	384
Prescreening Questions and Answers before the Job Interview	388
When the Recruiter Asks You the Prescreening Questions	389
Delay the Prescreening for another Day	390
Start Answering the Prescreening Questions on the Spot	391
When the Recruiter Emails You the Prescreening Questions	391
The Phone Interview	392
How Phone Interviews Benefit the Interviewers	393
How Phone Interviews Benefit Job-Hunting Candidates	394
How to Call In for a Phone Interview	394

Arrival at Your Job Interview — 395

    Arriving to a Job Interview at a US Government Agency on a Military Installation — 396

Introductions in Your Job Interview — 397

    When Staffing Agency Recruiters Meet You at Your Job Interview — 397

    When Staffing Agency Recruiters Do Not Meet You at Your Job Interview — 398

    Your Initial Greeting at Your Job Interview — 398

    The Hiring Manager in Your Job Interview — 399

    The Team Lead in Your Job Interview — 401

    When it's Your Turn to Give Your Introduction in Your Job Interview — 402

Intelligence Quotient (IQ) versus Emotional Quotient (EQ) for Job Interviews — 402

    The Importance of Intelligence Quotient (IQ) in Job Interviews — 403

    The Importance of Emotional Quotient (EQ) in Job Interviews — 405

    Even Presidents Go Through the Job Interview Process — 411

The Importance of Attitude in Your Job Interview — 416

Power Posture, Power Thoughts and Power Words for Job Interviews — 418

    How Posture Impacts Your Job Interview — 419

    How Power Thoughts and Power Words Impact Your Job Interview — 421

    Power Postures, Thoughts and Words—Use It or Lose It — 423

Other Factors That Impact Your Job Interview — 424

    How the Chair You're Seated On Impacts Your Job Interview — 424

    How Eye Contact and Head Level Impacts Your Job Interview — 425

    Where to Put Your Hands in Your Job Interview — 426

Job Interview Questions and Answers — 428

    The Interviewers that Ask the Questions — 428

    How to Answer Questions in Your Job Interview — 429

    How to Answer Questions about Salary in Your Job Interview — 431

    How to Answer Questions about How Soon Can You Start Working — 438

Questions to Ask the Interviewers and Closure — 439

    Closing Statements at the End of Your Job Interview — 440

    Thank the Interviewers for Inviting You to the Job Interview — 441

    Ask the Interviewers for the Job — 441

CHAPTER TEN: AFTER THE INTERVIEW—NOW WHAT? 443
   Congratulations! 443
   Sending Thank You Notes 444
   Perfecting Your Craft 446
   Other Job Opportunities 447
   The Wait and the Response 448
      What Happens If the Answer is No 449
      How to Handle Rejection after a Job Interview 451

CERTIFICATE OF ACHIEVEMENT 457
STRAIGHT FROM MY HEART 458
ABOUT THE AUTHOR 461

Introduction

In the 1999 American-Australian science fiction action film, *The Matrix*, we are introduced to Thomas A. Anderson portrayed by actor Keanu Reeves. During the respectable hours of his day job, Anderson worked in information technology (IT) as a computer programmer at a software company. During the discreet hours of the night, his true passion morphed his behavior that consumed his focus and lifestyle. In the dark seclusion of his humble rented apartment, he dons his black hat and goes by his computer hacker alias, Neo.

Underneath the skin of that unsatisfied double life that Neo lives, he's really no different than many of us in life today. Just someone who is curious, always searching, always believing there is something better for us out there in the world, in our future and our career.

Albert Einstein said, "*I have no special talent. I am only passionately curious.*"

At some point in our career, like Mr. Anderson, many of us find ourselves some place less than where we were meant to be; doing less than what we were meant to do; and making less money than we were meant to make. That's where we find Mr. Anderson as he tries to fit in as a "company man" in an IT corporation while somehow sensing he should be somewhere else.

Sound familiar? It should because many surveys, studies and reports show there's a long line of people calling it quits, job-hunting, job-hopping and changing careers among the rank and file across multiple industries in multiple countries.

Take for instance the report titled *Global generations: A global study on work-life challenges across generations*, a Harris Poll survey on behalf of EY (Ernst & Young), the third largest multinational professional services firm and one of the "Big Four" largest audit firms worldwide.

In this Harris Poll, 9,699 full-time working adults (ages 18–67) in different companies in eight different countries (US, UK, Germany, China, Japan, India, Brazil and Mexico) were surveyed between November 2014 and January 2015. Their research showed one-third of the full-time workers polled globally said their work and family life have grown increasingly more difficult to manage over the past five years.

What is the top reason for their struggles? Forty-nine percent of that lot said it was because their salary has not increased much while their expenses continue to rise. *Can I have an amen?* Of these 9,699 full-time workers polled, almost a third (31%) of these global employees changed jobs over their last five years.

In another Harris Poll on behalf of CareerBuilder, one of the most visited job search websites, 3,252 full-time non-government employees (ages 18 and over) were polled between November and December 2015.

This survey revealed almost a quarter of these employees (21%) pledged to leave their employers in 2016; an increase of 5 percent over 2014 (16%). *Pledge* is strong word when we're talking about quitting our job and abandoning our source of income and livelihood.

To pledge to leave your job is like saying, "*I can't wait to tell these folks at work, 'Take this job and shove it!'*"

The younger generation is leading the pack out their employer's doors in 2016 with almost a third (30%) employees ages 18–34 who planned to have a new job by the end of 2016; a 23 percent increase over 2014's Millennial Generation. Of these 3,252 full-time employees polled at the end of 2015, 34 percent were regularly searching for job opportunities, a 4 percent increase over the previous year (30%).

In the January 2016 *Job Openings and Labor Turnover* report by the Bureau of Labor Statistics (BLS), 2.8 million Americans quit their jobs across US government and private sectors over that single month of January. In April 2016, 2.8 million Americans quit their jobs; and in July 2016, 3 million Americans quit their jobs.

This BLS report is just a sampling of the fact that people are job-searching, leaving their jobs, job-hopping and changing their careers by the droves each month of the year. These figures include only those people who voluntarily quit their jobs, not people who left their jobs through retirement or involuntarily through layoffs or being fired from their jobs.

Even the actor Paul Marcarelli, who used to work for Verizon doing those famous *"Can you hear me now?"* commercials, has left Verizon and is now working for Sprint in 2016. As Marcarelli would say, *"Can you hear that?"*

Towards the opening scenes of *The Matrix*, Neo is standing in motionless submission in front of his boss' desk like a subordinate in military uniform standing at attention before his commanding officer. Beyond the privacy of his boss' office glass door is a sea of cubicles not unlike the cookie cutter cubicles in many offices in our 21st century workplaces. Both men are dressed in dark suit and tie, the dress code for their company.

Neo's boss, who is seated authoritatively at his desk, leans back snugly in his leather chair, taps his fingers on his desk while staring down Neo in a condescending manner and says, *"You have a problem with authority Mr. Anderson. You believe that you are special. That somehow the rules do not apply to you. Obviously, you are mistaken."* Then his boss gives Neo an ultimatum: *"The time has come to make a choice Mr. Anderson. Either you choose to be at your desk on time from this day forth or you choose to find yourself another job."*

Apparently, Neo's boss didn't read the BLS *Job Openings and Labor Turnover report.*

If you've been working in the job market for any length of time, you've experienced Neo's problem in the past; you're experiencing something similar in your job right now; or you'll come across this problem in the future. You know what that feeling is that comes with this problem? It's a gnawing feeling that says you deserve better than this—this pay, this job, this treatment, this working environment, this boss or this company. Things get to the point where you no longer enjoy working there but you have bills to pay. You are stuck there for the time being, consoling your aching heart and mind by telling yourself: ***It's only temporary; things will change; things will get better. I don't plan to be here forever.***

How do I know? Because I've been there too, and because these surveys and statistics I just quoted support what I'm describing.

Like Neo, during the respectable hours of our working day, our mind commanded us to stay at our position or our desk and keep coloring between the lines. However, in the secluded room of our heart's true passion, another person was taking shape and talking to us. Each day, that person morphed in our heart a little more. At first it was just a whisper but each day that voice grew louder and louder telling us: ***It's time to find another job***!

That feeling doesn't happen right away but it does happen. Like a marriage still buoyant on the "*I do's*" of wedding bells and hope-filled promises, the day eventually arrives when "*till death do us part*" unexpectedly creeps in to strangle what love and passion we had for that workplace. That job somehow lost its meaning and purpose in our lives. Just like Maverick sang to Charlie in the *Top Gun* film: "*You've lost that lovin' feeling*".

Laszlo Bock may not be one of The Righteous Brothers who originally performed the song *You've Lost That Lovin Feeling*, but he understands this principle of bringing meaning to people's workplaces. Bock heads Google's People Operations, and expounds upon this point of keeping that lovin' feeling in the workplace in his 2015 book, *Work Rules: Insights from Inside Google that Will Transform How you Live and Lead*.

That loss of meaningful purpose in their job is why so many working people have whispered complaints and expressed their frustrations to their co-workers, their families, their friends, to anyone who will listen. I know because I've been in their loveless shoes trudging through where they've been, and I've felt the nagging pain they felt about a job that, for one reason or another, has lost its lovin' feeling and sparkle in my eyes too.

If you've gone through this experience, you're not alone in feeling this way about jobs and workplaces. Everyone faces this demarcation line in their career where they have to decide whether to stay where they are in frustrated silence, like Neo, or start looking elsewhere and move on. There is nothing wrong or shameful about wanting to quit your job, search for another job, job-hop or change your career. Changing jobs is a healthy, natural growth process in everyone's career progression.

If you're in search of a job because you quit your job, were laid off, are changing careers, a first-time job seeker, recent grad, transitioning military veteran or someone who's returning to the workforce after a long absence; you're not alone in this journey and there's no cause for shame. You're among the ranks of **millions** of people each **month** (not each year; each month!) who are in search of a new job. Pull your shoulders back and hold your head up high with the rest of the crowd of job seekers.

You're going to get through this. You're going to come out on the other side better off than you were before. Have faith in yourself. Have faith in your God. And let the *Job Hunting Ninja Master* help you reach your desired goals for your career success.

When Steve Jobs, CEO of Apple Computer and Pixar Animation Studios gave his commencement speech to the 2005 graduating class at Stanford, he said, *"You've got to find what you love. And that is as true for your work as it is for your lovers. Your work is going to fill a large part of your life, and the only way to be truly satisfied is to do what you believe is great work. And the only way to do great work is to love what you do. If you haven't found it yet, keep looking. Don't settle. As with all matters of the heart, you'll know when you find it. And, like any great relationship, it just gets better and better as the years roll on. So keep looking until you find it. Don't settle."*

There's a Mr. Anderson in Every Workplace

In every job I've been in, there's always been someone like Mr. Anderson there who's lost that lovin' feeling. It's not long before you recognize Mr. Anderson on the job. He's the one at lunch who inevitably brings up his frustrations with work to you. During your break, she's the one in the breakroom telling you how things were so much better before at her last job. You can expect the Mr. Anderson at your workplace to do his usual drive-by dump of complaints at your desk, whispering a few words of discontent. At a side corner in the hallway, she won't hesitate to tell you what's wrong with this job. Sooner or later, the Mr. Andersons at your job are going to let you know they'd rather be working somewhere else.

As with every working person in both US government and private job sectors, you're either coming from a decision you made about a previous job; you're in the middle of making a decision about your current job; or you're on your way out because of the decision you made about your next job opportunity . . . again. Like Mr. Anderson, almost everyone knows what it's like to be at a crossroads where it's time to make a decision about their current job situation. They either stay at their job from this day forth or they choose to find themselves another job.

This is not an indictment against any workplace. Many employees are obviously happy and content to work there. They are oblivious to the ambitions of their co-workers who are about to launch themselves out of that place like an Olympic springboard diver who is aiming for high marks from the judges at the Rio Olympics.

I realize not everyone is frustrated with their workplace. Many people enjoyed their last job or they appreciate their current job. They are simply looking for something more in life; the next step in their career progression. Some people just need something more out of their job because of their goals and ambitions. They need a change. Some people know exactly what it is. Others haven't been able to put their finger on it as to what it is, where it is or how to go about finding it. They could use some help from someone who's already been through this dilemma called job transition. They need to talk to someone who has navigated successfully to the other side of this career coin and lived to talk about it.

Enter Morpheus

The first time we see Morpheus in *The Matrix*, played by actor Laurence Fishburne, he's offering Neo some choices about his current job and life dilemmas. Morpheus pries open a small metal container and pulls out two pills, one in each closed fist in front of Neo like a magician ready to perform a magic trick in front of an audience member.

Morpheus offers Neo this proposition: *"You take the blue pill and the story ends. You wake up in your bed and believe whatever you want to believe. You take the red pill; you stay in wonderland and I show you how deep the rabbit hole goes."*

Like Morpheus, I'm here to offer you some help about your career choices as you contemplate leaving your current job, increasing your salary, searching for a new job, job-transition, job-hopping or changing your career.

You can forget the advice I'm about to give you in this book; go about your life as usual; waking up in your bed each morning for the same job day in and day out; and believe whatever you want to believe about your world of available career opportunities.

Or you can continue reading and find out for yourself not only the possibilities but the realities of the wonderful land of job opportunities that await you. I'm going to show you how to have more control over the job search process that results in you having greater success in finding your next dream job at a higher salary. I'm going to reveal what your choices are in the job market and the advantages and disadvantages of those career decisions. I'm going to impart to you the secrets of successfully negotiating your salary and making it to your dream job on your terms. I'll show you how to have a slam dunk performance in your job interview as if you were one of those characters in the *NBA Jam: On Fire Edition* video game. You'll come out of your interview singing *Boom shakalaka!*

I'm going to show you how deep this job market rabbit hole goes. I will share with you inside information that recruiters, hiring managers and HR people don't want you know. Information that will allow you to make the kind of money you only dreamed of making in your career.

How much money am I talking about? How does a six-figure salary sound to you? That's the type of annual salaries I ask for and get in today's job market; and so can you. I didn't start at a six-figure salary in my career. Like so many others, I started out making minimum wage but over the years I learned the secrets to success. Many of my colleagues I've worked with in past jobs will never earn a six-figure salary because they never learned what I'm about to teach you in this book.

It's not because I'm the smartest or most experienced person in a room full of geeks or nerds. Some might say I'm a couple pancakes shy of a full stack. I only hold a bachelor's degree; not a master's or Ph.D.; and yet, I continuously command six-figures in salary negotiations. It's because I've learned some of the most effective and practical ways to get top dollar for my skill sets after years of searching for jobs, negotiating my salaries, and interviewing for jobs in both US government and corporate sectors. Whether you have limited education or hold a Ph.D., this information should be good news to you because it means you too can attain a six-figure salary.

If you're not making a six-figure salary in your job right now and you want to make that kind of money, I'll show you what it takes to get you there. I've been on the other side of that job-hunting and salary negotiation coin. I've seen what's on the other side. I've been a success at it; and like Morpheus, I'm back to show you the way there too. I'll help you navigate your way through the maze to the tremendous opportunities that are available to you in this job industry matrix we all call the US government and corporate job sectors.

What's my name? I'm the ***Job Hunting Ninja Master***.

CHAPTER ONE

Something for Every Job Seeker

If you haven't found it yet, keep looking.
Steve Jobs

In every bustling metropolis is a crowded chessboard of streets orchestrated with marching bands of vehicles playing never ending tunes of engine noise and honking drivers. Endless sidewalks are paved with the fluctuating sea of people ebbing and flowing in and out of shops, cafes and businesses. In these concrete jungles, there's bound to be buskers, more commonly referred to as street performers. These guitar playing, drum beating musicians, singers, magicians, jugglers and other entertainers amuse, delight and help pass the time away for meager monetary rewards or other gratuities to satisfy their thirst and hunger.

We oftentimes look down upon these one-man bands, sketchers, mimes, and other struggling artists and entertainers performing on these stages of street theaters as less advantaged than those of us who hold full-time or part-time jobs. But do you know one advantage these street performers have over the traditional working class?

CONTROL

They have complete control over when they work, how they work and where they work. And most important of all, they do it without having to pay taxes on their wages. We can learn something from street performers, especially when one of those street entertainers, Guy Laliberté, became the co-founder and former CEO of Cirque du Soleil, and has a 2016 net worth of $1.31 billion.

No, I'm not suggestion you strap on a pair of clown pants along with that tie you received last Christmas, grab your boombox and microphone, and start singing karaoke style on a busy street corner somewhere. Instead, we'll look at what works in today's 21st century working society and what doesn't in finding jobs, landing interviews and getting hired for your next dream job.

Within this humble livelihood earned among street performers lies a key, a secret to success—it is **control**. You've heard the saying, ***knowledge is power***. Well, here's the other piece to that puzzle: ***power is control***. Whether you are building a relationship, building a business or building a nation; knowledge, power and control will give you the upper hand and leverage for success in every endeavor in life. The same holds true in building your career.

Imagine where successful people like Bill Gates, Steve Jobs or Mark Zuckerberg would be if they didn't break free from the confines of their limited status quo and conventional wisdom and take control of their lives, their careers and their future? Meghan Trainor can sing to you all she wants that ***it's all about that bass***. Gates, Jobs and Zuckerberg would tell you that it's all about ***knowledge, power and control***.

Knowledge, power and control shape the outcome of success in whatever you are trying to achieve in life, whether you are a street performer or a CEO. This truth also applies to searching for and finding your next dream job, negotiating your salary to get top dollar for your skill sets, and convincing hiring managers and interviewers to hire you.

In this book, I'm going to provide you the knowledge and information that will give you the power to control the outcome of your job search. What outcome can you expect from this information?

SUCCESS!

No more trying to do what feels like a tightrope walk across Niagara Falls in the middle of the night with hurricane winds rushing at you from all sides every time you have to search for a new job. We're going to turn on the lights, plant your feet on solid ground, and safely lead you by the hand while we dance our way across that yellow brick road to your new job that awaits you in Emerald City. You're no longer in Kansas, Dorothy. This is the road to success!

Life is a Competition

So much in life is a competition. We compete for love and attention. We compete in war, in politics, in religions and philosophies. We compete in sports, in entertainment, in social media, in traffic and for the remote control. We compete with siblings while growing up. We compete in school during formal education. Then we compete for jobs throughout our working life.

Like it or not, job-hunting is a competition. Some people are in it to win it. Some want to avoid it, but can't. Others are just spectators, watching from the sidelines. Eventually, we all have to compete at one point or another in this activity called the job search.

The job search process is a competition between job seekers trying to find jobs; a competition between job recruiters trying to place job candidates in jobs; and a competition between employers trying to find people to fill job openings.

Like so many other competitions, the person who masters the proper technique of the competition wins. Mastering any technique requires good coaching, good mentoring, good knowledge, good advice and good practice. Job hunting is no different. That's what led you to this book. You're searching for the knowledge that will give you the power and control that will lead you to success in the job search process.

What you need is a master at this craft of job hunting. You need a sensei (*teacher*)—you need a *Job Hunting Ninja Master*.

Many people will pay thousands of dollars for the right mentor. Attendees to a Tony Robbins seminar could pay anywhere from $650 for a general admission ticket to $2,995 for a Diamond Premiere ticket. Other people will learn from the tuition-free school of hard knocks (which oftentimes turns out to be more expensive than a Tony Robbins seminar ticket). But you've chosen the best way, the most cost effective way to learn—reading this book.

What if you could learn from someone who's mastered the proper technique in the job search process to make you a success in your career regardless of what your job is? What if you could sit under the tutelage of someone who's been there; experienced it and succeeded at it? Think of how much time, energy and money you could save; how much pain you can avoid; how much money you could earn; and how much success you could achieve. All you need is the right teacher.

In competition, everyone experiences the thrill of victory and the agony of defeat. Everyone wins and losses in this competition called life. Everyone falls and rises in the process of learning. But why lose or fall when you can learn from someone else who has been through both—the failure and the success—and has mastered the technique of success?

Sure, we've all heard the saying: *What doesn't kill you makes you stronger*. But why flirt with something that can kill you and your chances for success if you don't have to?

Let the *Job Hunting Ninja Master* teach you instead.

The Warm-Up before the Competition

As we jump into the nuts and bolts of the job search process, which ultimately means more dinero in your pocket, let's first take a look at some things you may be unknowingly choosing for yourself whenever you search for a job or accept a position. These areas impact the type of job you have beyond the obvious job title and job description.

By understanding what you stand to gain and lose in these areas, you'll make more informed career decisions before you even start your job search or negotiate your salary or sign a job offer letter. After reading this section, you'll have greater knowledge and control over your job-searching efforts; something you can use to your advantage throughout your working life. If you haven't weighed the advantages and disadvantages of these areas before, you might be missing out on money, benefits and opportunities that are available to you. Last but not least, this information will help you wisely and confidently negotiate a higher salary or hourly rate with recruiters, human resource personnel and hiring managers.

Let's start your training.

You've probably heard the saying that the best time to look for a job is when you still have one. It's true. If you're in a job, and you know it's time to move on, start looking for your new job while you are still employed. Unencumbered with diminishing resources on top of mounting debt and bills, employed people have more time and liberty on their hands to search for that next dream job within the comfort zone of next week's paycheck. On the other hand, if you are among the unemployed crowd who are looking for work, do not fret. This book is your answer to the smartest and fastest way to finding and landing your next job.

But let's not just find you your next job. Let's give you the knowledge, power and control to put you in the best possible position for making the most money you've ever made in your career. I'll show you how to keep increasing your salary each time you look for a new job. It all begins with knowing a few things first. We'll start with the differences between employees and contractors.

Employees and Contractors

What made you choose to be a company employee instead of a contractor? How did you end up being a contractor instead of a company employee? Have you ever considered the circumstances or reasons that led to your decision to work in the employee or contractor workforce you're a part of today? You may have planned this out carefully or maybe you just fell into this career direction without giving it much thought.

The US government has given your employee and contractor status a lot of thought. So much thought that the government not only defines what are an employee and contractor, they figured out a way to tax that definition. Go figure; no surprise there. The government's decision on how employees and contractors are classified has an impact on the amount of money is in your paycheck each payday.

The Internal Revenue Service (IRS), the Fair Labor Standards Act and common-law rules define whether a worker is an employee or contractor. Employers have the power to hire an employee or contractor, but employers don't define what is an employee or contractor. The IRS uses common-law rules to determine if a worker is an employee or a contractor for taxation purposes. I know you'd like to put those two things—IRS and taxes—in a hot tub time machine and blast them up that government department where the sun don't shine. But stay with me for now and I guarantee you'll enjoy this quick ride through time.

Common law that the United States uses today originated from ancient laws of England during the Middle Ages that started out as societal and common customs and later became judgements and decrees enforced by law. In US courts today, common-law decisions are based on prior judicial decisions, called precedents, dating back to 5th century England's ancient laws. It is these common-law rules (precedents) on employment passed down through the ages that the IRS uses today in determining tax liabilities of employers, employees and contractors like you and me. (Apparently, the IRS has already taken that ride on the hot tub time machine—all the way back to the 5th century. Unfortunately for us, they didn't stay there.)

Common-law rules classify a worker as either an employee or contractor based on the level of **control** an employer has over the worker. If the employer controls the work to be done, how it will be done, as well as the results; and supplies the majority of the equipment, supplies, resources, training and direct compensation to the worker to complete the work; then the worker is considered an employee. In this case, the IRS would require the employer to withhold state and federal taxes before paying the employee their wages each payday.

When the employer lacks these elements of control over the worker, the worker is considered a contractor. In this case, the IRS does not require the employer to withhold state and federal taxes before paying the contractor their wages. Not so fast with the Snoopy dance if you're thinking about becoming a contractor to avoid paying taxes to the IRS. The IRS would seek these taxes directly from the contractor at the end of the tax year.

Independent Contractors versus Dependent Contractors

There are basically two types of contractors: independent contractors and dependent contractors.

Independent contractors are self-employed individuals that own their own business. Employers, customers and client payers do not pass the "common-law employer control test" with these contractors because independent contractors maintain the majority of control over the work they do, how their work is done and their resources. Once an employer, customer or client pays an independent contractor their "tax-free" wages for their products or services, the IRS would require the independent contractor—not the employer, customer or client—to pay state and federal taxes on those wages.

Dependent contractors on the other hand do not own their own business and are not self-employed. These contractors typically work for another company. Dependent contractors can work for either primary companies or secondary companies.

- **A primary company**, referred to as the "prime" company, is where the contractor works directly for the company that has the business need that the contractor is hired to fill.

- **A secondary company**, referred to as the sub-company or "sub", is where a contractor is hired by a secondary (sub) company to fill the business needs of a primary (prime) company.

An example of this second type of dependent contractor would be a secondary company, such as Lockheed Martin, working as a sub-company to a primary company such as Northrup Grumman. In this case, all of the contractors working for Lockheed Martin would be considered subcontractors or contractors working for the sub-company; and all the contractors working for Northrup Grumman would be considered contractors of the primary or prime company.

Another example of this second type of dependent contractor is staffing agencies. A staffing agency is a secondary company that oftentimes pays the salaries for contractors that are working for a primary company, also referred to as the company client or simply the client.

Primary company employers do not pass the common-law employer control test when using dependent contractors whose salaries and benefits are being paid by a secondary company or staffing agency. In this case, the primary employer would not withdraw state and federal taxes from the contractor's wages. The secondary company would withdraw those state and federal taxes from the contractor's wages each payday.

The secondary company or staffing agency paying contractors their salary and benefits pass the common-law employer control test over their contractors. Therefore, the secondary employer or staffing agency would have to maintain and keep track of all financial records on the contractor, including taxes withdrawn from their wages. This secondary company is required to submit a record of the contractor's wages and taxes withheld to the IRS. These records can also be audited by the IRS. This is the case when the contractor is working under W-2 and W-4 tax forms I'll briefly explain later.